For my friend and pilot Abe Ames: may dreams of jets come true for you.
—L.S.H.

This book is available in two editions:
Library binding by Lerner Publications Company, a division of Lerner Publishing Group
Soft cover by First Avenue Editions, an imprint of Lerner Publishing Group
241 First Avenue North
Minneapolis, MN 55401 U.S.A.

Website address: www.lernerbooks.com

Words in **bold type** are explained in the glossary on page 30.

Library of Congress Cataloging-in-Publication Data

Hill, Lee Sullivan, 1958–
    Jets / by Lee Sullivan Hill.
        p.   cm. – (Pull ahead books)
    Includes index.
    Summary: Introduces jet planes, how they work, and for
what purposes they are used.
    ISBN: 0–8225–1541–5 (lib. bdg. : alk. paper)
    ISBN: 0–8225–2383–3 (pbk. : alk. paper)
    1. Jet planes–Juvenile literature. [1. Jet planes.] I. Title.
II. Series.
TL547.H54 2005
629.133'349–dc22   2003020269

Manufactured in the United States of America
1 2 3 4 5 6 – JR – 10 09 08 07 06 05

Look! What's way up high?

It's a jet! It speeds across the sky and
leaves a cloudy tail.

ROARRRR. Jets zoom.

Thousands of jets fly every day. Some
hold boxes and cargo. The Beluga has
lots of room.

Three helicopters fit inside!

Some jets carry people. The Boeing 737 carries more than a hundred passengers.

The Boeing 747 is huge. People go
upstairs and downstairs inside it.

Learjets are small but quick.

Concordes fly even faster. Triangle-shaped wings cut through the air. They are called **delta wings.**

The F-14 jet flies super-fast. It flies up high with delta wings. And guess what? The wings move!

The pilot can make the wings stick out straight. This makes it easier to take off and land.

Pilots fly jets from the **cockpit.**

The pilot moves parts on the wings
called **ailerons.** They help tilt the jet
so it can turn.

The **rudder** stands up straight on the jet's tail. It helps turn the jet. On the tail wing, the **elevator** helps steer the jet up or down.

The pilot puts down **landing gear** to land. The wheels roll over the ground.

Pilots fly many kinds of jets. Harriers can fly almost straight down to land.

Pilots fly the U-2 up high. They take spy pictures of roads and buildings far below.

Pilots in Prowlers try to find the enemy. They go slowly like a cat looking for a mouse.

The B-2 can fly around the world. But won't it run out of **fuel**?

Not when a tanker jet flies by. It fills
fuel tanks through a long pipe. This jet
is like a flying gas station.

Most jets get fuel on the ground.
Fill it up!

Fuel makes **engines** run. The engines
make the jet fly. Can you find the jet
engines? They are under the wing.

Fuel burns inside jet engines. Hot air explodes out the back. The burst of air shoots the jet forward.

The engines roar. The jet zooms down
the **runway.**

Up, up and away!

Facts about Jets

■ Almost a million jets take off and land at Chicago's O'Hare airport each year.

■ A British and French team built the Concorde. It whisked people from New York to Paris in about two hours. Flights ended in 2003.

■ Many jets have nicknames. The U-2 is Dragon Lady. The EA-6B is the Prowler. And F-14s are Tomcats, because they like to fight.

■ Delta wings get their name from a Greek letter. The Greek letter *delta* looks like a triangle and so do delta wings on a jet.

■ A jet flies in three directions. The front of the jet aims up or down. That is called pitch. The wings tilt side to side or roll. The whole jet swings left and right, called yaw. Pilots control all three directions at the same time!

Parts of a Jet

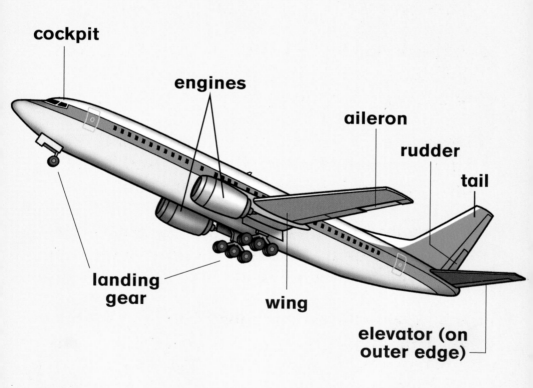

cockpit

engines

aileron

rudder

tail

landing gear

wing

elevator (on outer edge)

Glossary

ailerons: parts of the wing that help tilt the jet for turning

cockpit: the place where the pilot sits

delta wings: wings shaped like triangles

elevator: a part on the jet's tail wings that helps the jet go up and down

engines: the part that powers the jet and helps it fly

fuel: liquid that keeps the jet engine running

landing gear: wheels used when landing

rudder: a part on the jet's tail that helps the jet turn

runway: a place where a jet lands and takes off

Index

About the Author

Lee Sullivan Hill has written over twenty books for children. She lives with her husband and two sons in Illinois, halfway between Chicago's O'Hare and Midway airports. What does she like best about jets? She loves takeoff, when the jet picks up speed and races down the runway. Whoosh!

Photo Acknowledgments

The photographs in this book appear courtesy of: AIRBUS SAS, pp. 3, 6, 7; PhotoDisc Royalty Free by Getty Images, pp. 4, 27; Jeffrey Allen/U.S. Air Force, p. 5; © The Boeing Company, pp. 8, 9, 26; © George Hall/CORBIS, pp. 10, 16; © Bernard Weil/Toronto Star/ZUMA Press, pp. 11, 31; Felix Garza Jr./U.S. Navy, p. 12; Tyler Clements/U.S. Navy, p. 13; Arlo K. Abrahamson/U.S. Navy, p. 14; © Royalty Free/CORBIS, pp. 15, 24; © Stock Image/Super Stock, p. 17; David Senn/U.S. Navy, p. 18; Rose Reynolds/U.S. Air Force, p. 19; Michael B. W. Watkins/U.S. Navy, p. 20; Gary Ell/U.S.Air Force, p. 21; Kevin Robertson/U.S. Air Force, p. 22; Sean T. Blake/U.S. Navy, p. 23; Mark J. Rebilas/U.S. Navy, p. 25.
Cover image: © George Hall/CORBIS